D0810213

the art of
Simple
Living

how to enjoy the simple
things in life

An Hachette UK Company
www.hachette.co.uk

First published as 365 Ways to a Simple Spiritual Life
in Great Britain in 2005 by Godsfield Press, an imprint of
Octopus Publishing Group Ltd, Carmelite House,
50 Victoria Embankment, London EC4Y 0DZ
www.octopusbooks.co.uk

This edition published in 2019 by Pyramid, an imprint of
Octopus Publishing Group Ltd

ISBN 978-0-7537-3379-0

A CIP catalogue record for this book is available from the British Library

Printed and bound in China

10 9 8 7 6 5 4 3 2

For the Pyramid edition:
Publisher: Lucy Pessell
Designer: Lisa Layton
Editor: Sarah Vaughan
Production Controller: Grace O'Byrne

the art of
Simple
Living

how to enjoy the simple
things in life

introduction

In these pages you will find many ways to inspire you on your path
to a simpler life. Obviously some ideas and practises will speak to
you more than others, but I hope you will find all of them helpful
in some way. This little guide covers a vast range of topics, from
exploring your spirituality and your values to eating healthy and
inexpensive food.

You will find inspiration to help you define your own values
and to nurture your heart and soul. I've found that, if you want
to simplify your life and master the art of living, just about
everything – from the profound to the practical – has to be on
the table. We live in the most complex culture in history, and we
probably experience more activity and devour more information
in one day than our ancestors did in a lifetime. And all this takes
place in an intense electromagnetic haze of marketing, advertising
and entertainment. We may have acquired a lot of 'stuff' and
lead very stimulating lives, but real happiness and contentment
are often eluding us. In fact, countless numbers of us are sleep-
deprived, over-extended and deeply in debt; and stress-related
diseases are rampant. Somewhere along the line we have confused
standard of living with quality of life. And clearly they are not
the same.

Like many of us, I woke up one day admitting that I wasn't really happy with my life. I felt stressed and overwhelmed. I decided there must be a better way to live.

The road to a balanced and spiritual life is different for each of us. We have to look inside and ask ourselves: What makes me truly happy? What qualities do I want to embody? How do I want to feel – emotionally, physically and spiritually – on a daily basis? What work would be most fulfilling, regardless of the pay cheque? Are my possessions serving me or burdening me? How can I feel more connected to nature, to the people in my life and to my spiritual practice? What do I need to heal?

When you find your answers, they will provide you with a blueprint for a life that's no longer driven by external pressures. You will have set your life on a course that is internally guided by your highest motives and deepest values, and which is uniquely and authentically yours.

how to use this book

In reading this book, follow your nose and see what speaks to you and what doesn't. Feel free to read this book from front to back, back to front, or simply to open a page every day to see what jumps out at you. If possible, start a journal to keep track of the actions you take and any insights that you have about yourself or your lifestyle. List resources that you find on your own. Keep track of improvements in your sense of well-being and overall happiness. Note any difficulties and resistance that you may be experiencing and try to explore the causes. Lastly, find a support group. You may want to live a simpler, more spiritual life, but may find it difficult to swim against the swift current of social pressure. In other words, your friends and family may not understand what you're doing.

We are all unique individuals, on our own journey, but we are also social animals — we need the support of others. Check on the Web for 'simplicity support groups' in your area. You are, and always will be, a work in progress. Commit to simplifying your life and mastering the art of living, and you will begin an exciting, lifelong journey that will put you firmly in control of your own destiny. Take your time and, by all means, be kind to yourself. As my former teacher Gehlek Rimpoche advises, 'Don't bite off more than you can chew.' Good luck on your journey.

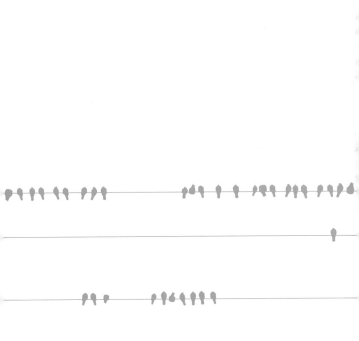

recognize things
as they are

Things are as they are. Looking out into the universe at night, we make no comparisons between right and wrong stars, nor between well and badly arranged constellations.

Alan W. Watts, philosopher and author

One of the most profound ways to simplify your life is to stop wanting things and people to be different from the way they are.

If you give up judging and resisting, you may fear that you will become a doormat, without aspirations or strong emotions. But what you gain is a loving heart, from which you can deeply, compassionately and joyously engage with life and others.

8

Think of a difficult relationship in your life. Experience your resistance to whatever makes this relationship problematic. Then imagine letting go and accepting this person just as he or she is. Which state of mind feels better?

don't be a consumer

**Is consuming the essence of who we are? It would seem not.
For most of our existence we were makers, not consumers ...**

Matthew Fox, spiritual theologian

Shopping is part of our modern way of life. But it's
important to remind yourself that you are not a consumer.
Your importance as a human being is not measured
by your buying power, or by the sophistication of your
carefully researched choices. Your value is not measured
by the cut of your clothes, by the car you drive or by the
brand of anything you buy.

For one week, don't go shopping. Try creating something
instead. You could plant your own herbs, write a poem,
make a drawing or bake something from scratch. Let go of
being a passive consumer and embrace yourself as a maker
and a creative being.

take a Japanese bath

In the West, a bath is a place one goes to cleanse the body.
In Japan, one goes there to cleanse the soul.

Bruce Smith and Yoshiko Yamamoto, authors of The Japanese Bath

Every evening without fail, millions of people lower
themselves gently into the steaming waters of a Japanese
bath. Whether it is a natural hot spring or a small tub at
home, this daily ritual remains an integral part of Japanese
life. With a little imagination, you too can add a deeply
satisfying evening soak to your daily routine.

Start by cleaning the bath and putting away any bathroom
clutter. Light some candles. Shower with soap and rinse
yourself; then fill your bath with hot water. Get in and sink
down up to your neck. Just relax … Vow to make time in
your life for this ancient and therapeutic pleasure.

gaze at the stars

Be glad of life because it gives you a chance to love and to work and to play and to look up at stars.

Henry Vandyke, author and Presbyterian minister

Throughout history the panoply of stars has drawn the eyes of humans skywards. We give them names, see pictures in their random placements and even navigate our world by their light.

But, in our citified ways, we live mostly indoors and, more often than not, get our experience of nature via our glowing TVs. If we do chance to look skywards, the glare of street lights may hide the awesome beauty above.

It's time to join your ancestors in a bit of star-gazing. Pick a clear night, grab a blanket and head for as dark an area as you can find. Let your mind flow among the patterns. Delight in the occasional shooting star or blinking satellite. Allow yourself to 'fall' into the vast night sky above.

use dreams for guidance

Both dreams and myths are important communications from ourselves to ourselves.

Erich Fromm, psychologist

Every night we have the opportunity to tap a goldmine. The goldmine is the world of our dreams. It's here that we can find guidance, learn about ourselves, solve problems and gain insights.

Before you go to sleep, set the intention to remember your dreams. Place a notebook and pen next to your bed, and in the morning write down everything you can recall. Do this for at least a week until you create the habit of remembering. Treat every aspect of the dream as a fascinating aspect of yourself. If a bird appears in your dream, be the bird. Or have a dialogue with the main person in your dream. Be open to both the positive and the negative, as your unconscious can be a tremendous resource for understanding your life. Let your dreams become an ally and a guide.

practise kindness

Constant kindness can accomplish much. As the sun makes ice melt, kindness causes misunderstanding, mistrust and hostility to evaporate.

Albert Schweitzer, theologian, physician and missionary

You may want to be kind, but you may have a habit of putting yourself first. An antidote to self-cherishing is to consider others to be as important as yourself. In doing so you are better able to respond appropriately to their needs. Practising kindness, then, becomes much easier and can even become a way of life.

On a daily basis, commit to at least one kind act each day. It could be as simple as giving a hug, sharing your home-grown tomatoes or calling a sick friend. If you want to take on kindness on a bigger scale, volunteer to work for a non-profit-making organization in your community. Practising kindness helps others and will make you happy as well.

nourish your friendships

Close friends contribute to our personal growth. They also
contribute to our personal pleasure, making the music sound
sweeter, the wine taste richer, the laughter ring louder because
they are there.

Judith Viorst, novelist and poet

Our friendships can be the most nourishing and sustaining
relationships of our lives. Yet our cultures often rank our
marriage partner, our parents or our siblings as more
important. Without thinking, we can subtly devalue our
friendships when they may, in fact, be the most crucial
ingredient in our sense of well-being and happiness.

Make a list of those people in your life whom you consider
to be friends. Do you sometimes feel more intimate with
your friends than with anyone else in your life? Honour
them by letting them know how much they mean to you.
Nourish your friendships by making time for friends in
your life.

go home

Home is where one starts from.

T. S. Eliot, poet

Home can mean many things. We yearn to 'go home' – wherever that may be. We get 'homesick'. With some people we feel more 'at home' than with others. We want our house or apartment to 'feel like home'.

What does home mean to you? Do you feel at home in your body? Do you yearn to come home to yourself? Spend some time writing about what 'home' means to you. If you don't feel at home in your physical dwelling, in your job, your relationship or your city or town, ask why that is so. What changes do you need to make in order to feel at home in your body, your mind and your physical surroundings?

get rid of guilt

Guilt agonizes over trifles, ignores wrongdoing.

Mason Cooley, aphorist

Guilt is a useless emotion. You can become stuck in guilt and shame, and even make it part of your identity. Yet it doesn't necessarily lead you to change your behaviour or make you a better person. Regret, on the other hand, is a more positive emotion. It allows you to focus on your actions, and moves you towards change and healing.

First, if you caused someone harm, acknowledge it. Then express sincere regret for having hurt them. Let them know this is not the way you want to behave. If possible, do something to make amends. Ask the person what you can do to make things better. And then commit to yourself, and to them, that you will refrain from that harmful behaviour in future. Allow yourself to feel purified and renewed by this process.

create a garden
for your soul

I know a little garden-close, set thick with lily and red rose, where I would wander if I might from dewy dawn to dewy night.

William Morris, poet

You can plant flowers or tomatoes, mow the lawn and get your ivy to climb. Gardening can be just another weekend chore – or it can feed your soul and your imagination.

Assess the state of your garden – whether it's a few clay pots on a balcony or a generous expanse behind your house. What would make your garden magical, whimsical and a delight to your soul? Is it colour, fragrance, places to walk and shady places to meditate? Or is it herbs and vegetables, which have personalities of their own? If you are going to take the time and expense to make a garden, then have a relationship with its inhabitants and enjoy its spirit. Tend it lovingly and use it to soothe your soul. Make it a sacred place for joy, peace and prayer.

remember to rest

Everywhere I have sought rest and not found it, except sitting
in a corner by myself with a little book.

Thomas à Kempis, monk and mystic

You've heard it often: that it's important to rest. You'll get
to rest, you say, if there's time to rest. But ignore the need
for rest at your peril. For it is by resting that you rejuvenate
your body and mind.

During rest you may have your best insights and gain
perspective on the frantic activity that has become the
norm of modern life. Rest is essential to all creatures and
all activities. It is integral to a musical score, a painting or
a performance. In art there is always the play of movement
and non-movement, activity and non-activity. The places
of rest define and illuminate.

Do you get enough rest? Do you value rest as much as you
do activity? How would your life change if you did so?
After reading this, close your eyes and take a nap.

meditate on your breath

Through meditation and by giving full attention to one thing at a time, we can learn to direct attention where we choose.

Eknath Easwaran, spiritual teacher

Meditation on the breath is an ancient method to calm the mind. To begin, sit cross-legged on a cushion or, if that's not possible, on a chair. Keep your spine straight and, if you're sitting on a chair, keep both feet flat on the floor. Cradle your right hand in your left and rest both loosely against your navel. Focus your eyes about 1m (3ft) in front of you.

Now pay attention to your breath as it enters and leaves your nostrils. Count your breaths up to ten, using the out-breath, then start again. Acknowledge any thoughts that arise and return immediately to your breath. Do this for ten minutes. Notice how often your mind strays from attention on your breath. Did you realize your mind was so active? Is there a pattern to your thoughts?

keep a journal

I am carrying out my plan, so long formulated, of keeping a journal … and thus I shall improve myself.

Eugène Delacroix, artist

One of the best ways to help yourself is to write in a journal on a daily basis. Try writing down your thoughts and feelings about whatever is bothering you.

If you're having trouble with a friend or a spouse, use your journal to explore the issues. Attempt to understand their perspective by writing from their point of view. If you have to make a big decision, write down the pros and cons and further explore your thoughts. If you want to savour a special moment, record it in your journal. If you have spiritual insights, express them. Try writing your journal first thing in the morning. Articulating what's in and on your mind should free you to get on with your day.

learn to listen

**It is the disease of not listening, the malady of not marking,
that I am troubled with.**

William Shakespeare, dramatist and poet

Here's an old joke: in Hollywood, there are only two things
– talking and waiting to talk. You may not be a movie
star, but you too may have trouble listening. It takes effort
to listen. More to the point, it takes an open mind and
heart. That may be difficult for you to achieve. You may
have a hard time trusting and want to protect yourself.
Or perhaps no one listened to you when you were a child.
However, through active listening, you gain the joy of deep
communication with another human being. You may learn
something valuable. And you may help someone to speak
the truth.

Practise the art of listening by focusing your attention on
the other person. Before you respond, let them know you
have heard and understood what they've said.

use the Web mindfully

You affect the world by what you browse.

Tim Berners-Lee, inventor of the World Wide Web

The World Wide Web and its big cousin, the Internet, create a world of extraordinary connections. What you choose to browse, and where you surf to on the Web, helps create the Web itself. If you set up your own site, you're offering it to hundreds of millions of Web users.

Because the Web is one big dynamic universe, it's important to keep your energy positive. Don't surf to negative websites, and don't create them, either. Be mindful of the quality of your communications. Energetically, you're now connected to millions of people around the world, so be careful how you contribute to that universe.

appreciate what
you have

Think not on what you lack as much as on what you have.

Greek proverb

The trick to having a positive mind, even in the worst
of times, is to focus on what's going right for you. When
you feel you don't have everything you need, it's easy to
discount your blessings. When you don't have money for
the rent, and the bills are piling up – even though it may be
difficult – focus on what you do have. Be sure to consider
non-material wealth: your family and friends, your health,
your education, your talents and your values. Then focus
on the material wealth you do have (however small).

Even if you are wealthy, it's easy to focus on what you don't
have. Regardless of your situation, always appreciate what
you do have. This positive outlook will transform your life.

simplify your wardrobe

Simplicity, simplicity, simplicity!

Henry David Thoreau, essayist, poet and naturalist

If you work in an office, you probably have to look good every day, and this can consume your hard-earned money. If your clothing budget is eating into your salary, first consider having a simpler wardrobe.

Classic styles in solid colours can help you look presentable for work in half the time, and they last from season to season. If you have tops and bottoms that mix and match, you'll make a few pieces go a long way. Be sure to buy khaki, black and white, and then build from there. Women: use scarves and jewellery to change your look. Men: use ties and coloured shirts. Also, try buying women's or men's business suits at a second-hand clothing shop. The cost savings are significant.

work with joy

And no one shall work for money, and no one shall work for fame, but each for the joy of the working.

Rudyard Kipling, writer and poet

We work primarily for an income. Yet we also work for the approval of others, for a sense of power and mastery, and to be of service to others. But how many of us work to experience joy? It's not so much what you do as how you do it that's the key to joyful work.

Be fully present, at each moment, as you go through your day. You can do this by bringing all your senses and awareness to each task. In other words, regardless of pressure, focus only on what you are doing now. By doing so you'll be less reactive to external demands and interruptions, and more empowered in using your skills and knowledge. You'll also unleash your creativity and problem-solving abilities.

declare your interdependence

I am a part of all that I have met.

Alfred, Lord Tennyson, poet

If you are feeling alienated and alone, try meditating on the interdependence of all life. Consider that you are connected to all other living beings. You depend on others in countless ways and they depend on you. For instance, you depend on others to provide heat, light, electricity, health care, food, transportation, clothing, education, work, love and friendship – the list is endless. And you serve others in the same ways. You are also connected to all other sentient beings, and to all aspects of nature, both animate and inanimate.

You also depend on what you create with, and among, others. So your well-being – and the well-being of all – depends on your ability to create relationships that are balanced, loving and positive.

take your own lunch

There is no such thing as a free lunch.

Anonymous

Do you buy your lunch every day at work? If you do, you could be making a significant hole in your pay cheque. Of course, there are lots of reasons to do this; such as: 'Who has time to make lunch in the morning?'; 'My friends go out to lunch and I don't want to be anti-social'; and 'It's not trendy to bring a lunch box to work.'

Add up what you spend on lunches in a year. You may be in for a shock! How many hours did you work to pay for that daily expense? Now calculate how much it would cost to pack a simple lunch. Figure out the difference. How would you spend the money you would save? How about a holiday at the beach, or maybe a new computer?

wake up to time

Time is a sort of river of passing events, and strong is its current.

Marcus Aurelius, Roman emperor

You wear a watch to keep on schedule. You may buy books on time management. And complain that you're so busy you just don't have enough time in the day. You say, 'I need to find more time' or 'I need to make more time'. This suggests you have the power to create more of it whenever you need it. But do you really understand the dynamic quality of time?

Like a river, time flows on relentlessly, and each minute that passes is irreplaceable. Your days, weeks and months pass so quickly they can seem like a dream. Wake up to time in order to experience that each moment is precious. Wake up to time and you'll make better choices in how you live your life. Spend a few minutes each morning meditating on how you can best use your time today.

explore mentoring

A mentor's principal purpose is to help another develop the qualities he or she needs to attain his or her goals – without a mentor.

Shirley Peddy, author of The Art of Mentoring

Mentoring is a way to give and get life counselling. You can mentor a person by giving support, counsel, friendship and constructive example. Or you can have a mentor yourself. If you're trying to excel in a particular career, having a mentor can make all the difference.

Identify someone who is accomplished in something you want to do. Approach him or her for possible advice and counsel. If you both like each other, ask that the relationship be ongoing. If you want to be a mentor for a young person, search on the Web for organizations in your area that work with kids. Mentoring is a wonderful way to give to your community.

make a budget

The budget should be balanced.

Marcus Tullius Cicero, orator and statesman

Why make a budget? You may feel that you don't make enough money to make this worthwhile. But the less you have, the more you need a budget. If you're in debt and without savings, you definitely need one.

First, track your expenses for three months. When you have a picture of where your money is going, decide where you can cut back. Second, list all your debts. Third, create a budget for the next year by calculating your income and your fixed and variable expenses. Design your budget with relevant categories. Fourth, track your income and expenses and keep your budget up-to-date.

A budget is a financial tool for getting out of debt and increasing your financial wealth. It's also a tool for living a more conscious and balanced life.

go on a nature walk

The day I see a leaf is a marvel of a day.

Kenneth Patton, Christian minister and poet

Unless your job takes you outside, you probably spend a lot of time working and living indoors. But don't let your busy schedule deprive you of walking amid nature.

Check out what parks are available nearby. If you have a little more time, try to get out of the city. Give yourself at least an hour to walk in a garden or wooded area. When walking, try not to get lost in your thoughts. Instead, focus on your surroundings. Pay attention to the trees, the plants and flowers. How many can you name? Notice any animals, birds and insects, and examine their behaviour. Breathe deeply and experience the heady smells of the earth. Nature walks renew body and soul and are a great activity to share with children.

use stress-busters

Every stress leaves an indelible scar.

Hans Selye, physician and author

Stress takes its toll on our bodies and minds. So what can you do to counteract its effects? First of all, whatever you do, do it on a daily basis. Meditating or walking once a month isn't going to help. Second, spend a month exploring many different methods of stress reduction so that you can find out what works for you.

Are you a movement person? Then try walking, biking or Tai chi. Are you an exercise type? Then go for yoga. Do you love music? Then listen to one of the many music CDs made for relaxation; or, if you find voices soothing, try listening to a recorded guided meditation. If you need quiet, then find somewhere you can experience complete silence for 15 or 30 minutes each day. If you need self-expression, try painting, singing, writing or dancing.

eat in

I was 32 when I started cooking; up until then, I just ate.

Julia Child, cook and author

If you want to save some serious money, stop 'eating out' in restaurants. Instead, buy groceries and 'eat in'. If that sounds like a prison sentence, you may want to explore some of the positive reasons for cooking and eating at home.

First, you'll learn how to cook or be a better cook. Use your local library as a source of free cookbooks. Second, you can improve your health by controlling what and how much you eat. No more greasy fast food or huge restaurant portions. Third, you can enjoy gourmet meals without breaking the bank – recreate those special dishes at home. Fourth, you can enjoy low-cost socializing with friends by having pot-luck meals. Fifth, you can potentially save lots of money per year. Now, what's so bad about that?

33

be truthful

The good I stand on is my truth and honesty.

William Shakespeare, dramatist and poet

One of the best ways to simplify your life is to be honest. There's nothing more stressful than keeping track of stories you've invented or embellished. It may seem like a good idea, at the time, to alter the truth – you may want to protect someone from pain, or protect yourself from embarrassment; or maybe you're intending to give yourself an advantage and cheat in a test.

But, in the long run, if you are dishonest you complicate your life. And in the end you may cause more pain to yourself and others than if you had told the truth. Honesty is like a fresh breeze. The trick is to be simultaneously honest and kind.

redefine success

Success is an absurd, erratic thing.

Alice Foote MacDougall, businesswoman

Our culture's definition of success is fairly limited. The signs are mostly external: a high-paying job, a nice car, beautiful clothes, a beautiful partner and a large home.

Consider these alternative definitions of success, which don't require conspicuous consumption: you have a successful life if you have a safe place to live, good health, a nurturing family life, ongoing education, spiritual development, good friends, and work that feeds you emotionally and intellectually. You're a successful person if you are capable of giving and receiving love and experiencing joy.

What do you consider to be the ingredients of a successful life? More importantly, how do you measure success for yourself?

drink water

It is essential for the proper functioning of the body to drink
at least eight glasses of quality water each day.

James F. Balch, MD, author of Prescription for Nutritional Healing

Water is simplicity itself. And our bodies are two-thirds
water; the human brain is 95 per cent water, blood is 82 per
cent water and the lungs are nearly 90 per cent water. So
adequate water benefits nearly every human body function.

The benefits of drinking enough water are extensive, so
it is worth mentioning a few. Water removes toxins from
the body and helps with elimination. It aids digestion and
converting food into energy. It helps you lose weight, have
more energy and perform better. Staying fully hydrated
reduces headaches and dizziness. Drinking adequate water
decreases your chances of getting colon and bladder cancer.
And there are beauty benefits: your skin looks fresher and
younger. If you're addicted to sugary soft drinks, try pure
water as a healthy alternative.

exercise cheaply

Health is the vital principle of bliss, and exercise, of health.

James Thomson, poet

Gym and health-club memberships are expensive. It just takes a little thought and creativity to find an alternative.

Some suggestions are: ride your bicycle to work; walk short distances instead of driving; use the stairs instead of elevators; or do some gardening as a form of exercise. Check out your neighbourhood parks for walking and running tracks – some of them include stations for doing chin-ups or other exercises. And inexpensive exercise balls are great for home use. They help you improve your balance, coordination and core strength in your abdominals and back. If you want company when you exercise, check your local newspaper for details of walking, running and biking clubs.

simplify your kitchen

Your kitchen can quickly become overwhelmed with clutter. Over time, it's easy to collect utensils you don't use, food that's out of date and dishes that have never seen the light of your table. Having a clean, organized and efficient kitchen will encourage you to cook meals at home and save you money.

Start by emptying all your kitchen cabinets and drawers. Sort your dishes, pots, pans and utensils into piles – those that you want to keep, those that are broken or excessively worn and those that you can give to charity. Next, sort through your staples and condiments. Throw out the old stuff, including old spices. Get rid of any appliances you don't use. Finally, clean your cabinets inside and out and put back everything you want to keep.

get some sunlight

Be like the flower, turn your faces to the sun.

Kahlil Gibran, poet and philosopher

Sunlight is one of the most overlooked keys to good health. Unfortunately, too much living indoors, coupled with a fear of skin cancer, has kept us from enjoying its benefits.

Excessive exposure to the sun may cause skin cancer, but there is also evidence that sunlight helps prevent other forms of cancer, as well as heart disease and osteoporosis. Sunlight benefits your bones, lowers your cholesterol and blood pressure and wards off depression. Our bodies need 400 units of vitamin D a day – you can get that by exposing your face to sunlight for 15 minutes. We all feel better when the sun comes out. For better health, be sure to get a little sunlight each day.

practise silence

No spiritual exercise is as good as that of silence.

Seraphim of Sarov, Orthodox Christian saint

Find a way to be alone in a quiet place. Take a vow of silence for the next 24 hours. Don't speak a word or communicate with anyone in any way. Don't watch television or listen to your radio or CD player. Stay away from your computer, and unplug the phone and your bleeper. Turn off your mobile phone too. Do not read for distraction or entertainment.

Use this time to meditate, do yoga or take a bath. Write about silence and solitude and how they make you feel. Are you comfortable being alone without your normal distractions? Are you scared, bored, anxious or relieved? Do you find the silence nurturing and renewing? Let the silence provide an opening to explore the most fragile and tender parts of your soul.

turn off the television

Television should be kept in its proper place – beside us, before us, but never between us and the larger life.

Robert Fraser, former head of the British Independent Television Authority

Television has its redeeming values, but mostly it bombards us with images of conflict, violence and exploitation. Like moths drawn to the light, we sit mesmerized in front of the screen. The problem is: not only do our minds become dulled by the constant stimulation, but we begin to confuse this passive, vicarious activity with actual living.

Like most addictions, a television addiction can be hard to kick. Try cutting down gradually by substituting other activities that you find enjoyable. Have a family game night, take the dog for a walk in the park or read a book. Have days with no television. Limit your viewing time and intentionally choose what you want to watch.

start something new

Age is something that doesn't matter, unless you are a cheese.

Billie Burke, actress

Do you feel you're too old to start something new? Do you feel life has passed you by? Think again! American primitive artist Grandma Moses taught herself to paint in her late seventies. Selma Plaut earned her Bachelor's degree from the University of Toronto at the age of 100. George Dawson learned to read and write at 98, and wrote his autobiography, Life Is So Good, at 100. Tom Lane started swimming competitively at the age of 82. Centenarian comedians Bob Hope and George Burns kept us laughing until the end.

If you too want to live to be 100, accept change gracefully. Be a lifelong learner. Practise seeing the glass half full, and be eager to see what tomorrow brings. Most importantly, make new friends. No matter what your age, never stop pursuing your dreams.

heal with music

Music is the answer to the mystery of life.

Arthur Schopenhauer, philosopher

Music author and visionary Don Campbell became seriously ill with a blood clot behind his right eye. He used music to heal himself. His book *The Mozart Effect* came out of his own experience with the transformational and healing powers of sound and music. He believes that we can use music to improve our memory and awareness, enhance our listening and attention-deficit disorders, heal mental disorders and physical injuries, activate creativity and reduce depression and anxiety.

When you listen to music, does it relax or energize you, or leave you feeling jangled? Be aware of how it affects your mood and health. Explore music as a healing and creative force in your life.

think positive

Our belief at the beginning of a doubtful undertaking is the one thing that ensures the successful outcome of the venture.

William James, psychologist

Worry not only takes its toll on your health, but undermines all your activities. Fear and doubt create outcomes in line with your thinking. In other words, if you fear things won't work out successfully, then they probably won't. On the other hand, if you cultivate a positive outlook, your chances of enjoying positive outcomes increase.

List any current plans you may have – large or small, immediate or long-term. Examine your thinking about these ventures. Write down any negative thoughts or fears you may have. Counteract these pessimistic thoughts by visualizing and writing down positive outcomes. Try to practise positive thinking on a daily basis.

make a difference

If you think you're too small to make a difference, you haven't
been in bed with a mosquito.

Anita Roddick, entrepreneur and activist

You may say, 'One person can't make a difference, so
why bother?' But you can make a difference through
volunteering. Once you open your heart to the idea, there
will be no lack of opportunities.

Try teaching someone to read through a literacy
programme, or working with a troubled teenager
through your local school or church. And there are many
organizations worldwide that care for homeless.

Or if politics attracts you, dive in – work on an election, or
work with a non-governmental organization. You'll make a
difference for yourself and for others.

look at the sky

The sky is the daily bread of the eyes.

Ralph Waldo Emerson, author and poet

If you live in the country, you probably look at the sky every day. If you live in a city, you probably don't. Yet, if you're forgetting to look skyward, you're missing one of the glories of the universe.

The sky is exquisitely beautiful, its changeableness infinite, its colours breathtaking. Its clouds take on the shapes of birds, rabbits and menacing dragons, or envelop everything in a beautiful mist. They have great Latin names such as cumulus, stratus, cirrus and nimbus.

46 Give your mind a rest, and your soul some inspiration, by looking at the sky above for five minutes a day.

live in the now

No valid plans for the future can be made by those who have no capacity for living now.

Alan W. Watts, philosopher

Try sitting quietly for a few moments. Notice what thoughts appear. If you're like most mortals, you'll find yourself thinking of past events, or speculating about the future. It's difficult to be totally present and focused in the moment. But if you never dwell fully in the present your future will simply be a continuation of not living in the present. Only by making an effort to be in the present moment can you reliably know who you are and what you want.

Do this by using your senses. Take in what is around you, and notice how you feel. Make a practice of living in the now. Then use the insights you gain to plan your future. In this way your future will serve you well.

heal yourself
with laughter

If taking vitamins doesn't keep you healthy enough, try more laughter: The most wasted of all days is that on which one has not laughed.

Nicolas Chamfort, writer

When you laugh, you lower your blood pressure, reduce your stress and increase the oxygen levels in your blood, making you feel more energized. You also increase your endorphin levels, which makes you feel great. Laughter even gives your muscles a workout.

If you're feeling down and you want to laugh, you have to make an effort. Watch a movie that you know makes you laugh, read the cartoons in the newspaper, watch a TV sitcom or sign up for a free joke service on the Internet. If you're upset about the state of the world, read some political satire. And when you read the morning paper don't skip the funnies. When it comes to your health, laughter is a serious business!

take a five-minute break

No matter how much pressure you feel at work, if you could
find ways to relax for at least five minutes every hour, you'd be
more productive.

Dr Joyce Brothers, psychologist and author

You may work for three or four hours at your computer
without getting up. When you finally stop, you're
exhausted. Your body is cramped, your shoulders are
slumped, your eyes are burning and your breathing is
shallow. Yet, although you may be working long hours, you
may not be as productive as you think.

Take five minutes out of every hour to stand up and
stretch. Then gently palm your eyes and rub your temples.
Take a few deep breaths, and if possible take a short walk.
You'll be much more productive, and healthier both
physically and mentally, at the end of the day.

improve your sleep

What we need to do is create bedrooms that are very serene,
restful and very good at getting us to relax.

*Terah Kathryn Collins, author of The Western School Guide
to Feng Shui*

The ancient Chinese art of feng shui is dedicated to
enhancing the environment and energy around you. If
you're having trouble sleeping, consider the following
feng shui advice.

First, remove the TV, computer and any exercise
equipment from your bedroom, to make the room as
serene as possible. If your bed is opposite a mirror, cover
the mirror with a cloth at night. Position your bed so that
you can see the door, but are not directly in front of it. Try
not to sleep next to a window. Place your bed against a
wall or use a solid headboard. Make sure there is nothing
hanging directly overhead, such as a light fixture, a ceiling
fan or a beam.

take a volunteer holiday

Never doubt that a small group of thoughtful citizens can change the world. Indeed, it is the only thing that ever has.

Margaret Mead, anthropologist

Many volunteer organizations around the globe provide opportunities for individuals, families or groups to spend their holiday volunteering their services to help others. Activities range from working on archaeological digs to restoring trails in national parks and counting wildlife. Most volunteer holidays cost less than going to the same location as a tourist and provide a more enriching experience. Service holidays are first and foremost about service, yet you'll always have some free time in which to explore on your own. Search for 'service vacations' or 'international volunteerism' on the Internet to find an organization offering a programme right for you.

pay attention

Life is denied by lack of attention, whether it be to cleaning
windows or trying to write a masterpiece.

Nadia Boulanger, musical composition teacher

Bringing your full attention to bear on whatever you're
doing is essential to all accomplishments, however lofty or
mundane. It's a skill that takes practice, and it's developed
with effort. Many self-help books recommend multi-
tasking – reading while you eat, watching television while
you cook, reading and answering emails while talking
on the phone. However, no one wrote a symphony while
making dinner.

Breathe deeply for a few moments before you begin a
task. Let go of all thoughts, except those that pertain to
what you are about to do. Bring all your intention to
focus on the work before you. Notice whether you feel
more interested in life when you practise single-minded
attention on the task in hand.

create your own ceremonies

When humans participate in ceremony, they enter a sacred space. Emotions flow more freely … All is made new; everything becomes sacred.

Sun Bear, Native American chief

We have modern-day celebrations such as birthday parties, weddings, graduations and festivals of all kinds. But we have lost the power of ritual and ceremony – practices that mark and elevate our transitions in life, that honour the seasons, that begin new ventures.

Consider creating your own rituals or ceremonies for yourself, and for your friends and loved ones. Start by creating a ceremony for the next transition in your life. If you have a new job, create a ritual with your partner or a friend, using symbolic objects, flowers, candles, incense and clothing. Express your intention for this new work to be spiritually, emotionally and financially rewarding.

start a reading group

Go three days without reading and your speech will become tasteless.

Chinese proverb

If you love to read, a great way to share your passion for reading is to start a reading group. Reading groups, or book clubs, are great ways to stay connected with friends, meet new friends and participate in your community.

Organize your reading group or book club according to genre (such as fiction or poetry) or subject matter (such as current events or spirituality). If you meet in members' homes, combine your meetings with pot-luck meals or dessert and coffee. If your group is larger, try reserving a room at your local church or library. Some book shops are happy to provide meeting space. To help build a strong group, keep the meeting time consistent and limit your discussion time to two hours.

embrace the mysterious

The most beautiful thing we can experience is the mysterious.
He to whom this emotion is a stranger, who can no longer
pause to wonder and stand rapt in awe, is as good as dead.

Albert Einstein, theoretical physicist

The mysterious attracts and pulls us like a magnet, yet its
meaning eludes us. Mystery takes us out of our literal mind
and into a world larger than ourselves. The mysterious
delights, frightens, stimulates, engenders awe and opens
our hearts.

Do you prefer to stick to the literal and the known, or
do you let yourself ponder the mysteries of life. Do you
wonder how far the universe extends? Or how we came
into being? Do you think about life after death, one of the
biggest mysteries of all? When you feel life is too small and
predictable, remember that life is full of mystery.

make clear choices

What we have to contribute is both unique and irreplaceable.
What we withhold from life is lost from life. The entire world
depends upon our individual choices.

Duane Elgin, author of Voluntary Simplicity

Think of your life as a series of choices. For every past
action, you made a choice, whether or not you were
conscious of making one. You may reflect on a past
situation and say, 'I had no choice, I had to do it.'
However, no matter how trapped you may have felt,
you made a choice.

You make choices hundreds of times a day, from the
inconsequential to the profound. Knowing that you're
choosing all your actions brings clarity, responsibility and
accountability to your life. Each evening, ask yourself if
your choices that day have contributed positively to your
life and to the universe.

stay curious

Never lose a holy curiosity.

Albert Einstein, theoretical physicist

You are born curious, with an open and questioning mind. But your enthusiasm may get squelched, at school and at work, where everyone seems to want answers instead of questions. It's time to reclaim the purity and innocence of your 'holy curiosity'. In a notebook, make a list of 50 questions that are important to you. Don't hesitate to sound naive. Ask 'Why is the sky blue?' if you want to. Pursue the answers to your questions.

Next, make a list of 50 things you would like to learn, if you had the opportunity. Do you want to try yoga, or become a firefighter? Write it down. Then choose one new skill and take a class. If you keep your curiosity alive, your life will be endlessly interesting.

have self-respect

Never violate the sacredness of your individual self-respect.

Theodore Parker, theologian, pastor and scholar

When you look in the mirror, do you have respect for the person staring back at you? Are you living your life with dignity, in line with the values you want to uphold? If you can't answer 'Yes', ask yourself why not. What would you have to do to regain your self-respect?

Perhaps you're doing work that pays well, but ultimately harms other people. If so, try to find more positive employment. If you're in a relationship that is demeaning, leave it. If you have an addiction, get help. If you harmed someone, make amends. Self-respect takes self-love, self-compassion and ongoing maintenance.

forgive

It is the act of forgiveness that opens up the only possible way to think creatively about the future at all.

Father Desmond Wilson, Catholic priest and activist

If you forgive, you may feel you have to swallow your pain or be vulnerable to further harm. But you can express your feelings, set healthy boundaries and forgive, regardless of what the other person feels, says or does.

Recall times when you have hurt others and have been glad of their forgiveness. Recognize that no one is perfect. If you know the person who has hurt you, forgive them, even if you end your relationship. If the person is a stranger, forgive them regardless of what they did. Not forgiving kills your compassion and keeps you frozen in the past. Forgiveness of others, and yourself, is essential if you are to move freely into your future.

keep playing

We don't stop playing because we grow old, we grow old because we stop playing.

George Bernard Shaw, dramatist

Play is not just for children, or even just for humans. Animals play in order to practise for the hunt, to socialize, to keep fit, to stay alert and to enjoy themselves. Watch crows: they will throw a twig and then swoop down and catch it. Children play to learn motor skills, to practise being adults and to experience joy. Adults need to play to be creative, to experience joy and continue to learn. Yet it's extremely easy to forget how to play.

How can you bring play back into your life? If you're feeling inhibited, start playing more with your own or other people's kids. Play with your pets. Be more playful with your partner. Try to bring the spirit of play into every day.

plant trees

A man has made at least a start on discovering the meaning of
human life when he plants shade trees under which he knows
full well he will never sit.

D. Elton Trueblood, cartoonist

You are not just a single individual, who lives and dies
separate from the rest of nature and humanity. On
the contrary, you are a citizen of the universe and are
energetically connected to all other beings. As a citizen of
the universe, and a resident of planet Earth, you are called
to be a steward of her resources for those living in the
present, and for future generations to come.

Consider planting a tree every year, that others might
enjoy them after you've gone. Thinking of your life in this
connected, expanded and responsible way – and acting
on that understanding – enhances your time here on Earth
and, in time, may help you deepen your understanding
of reality.

pay attention to
the moon

**Right down to the level of individual cells, the lunar wind is
blowing and bringing all living creatures into vibrant motion.**

Johanna Paungger, author of Moon Time

When the moon is new (or dark), set your intention for
something you would like to manifest – perhaps healing
for yourself or someone else, or a new relationship. As the
waxing crescent appears in the night sky, see this as the
first sign of the manifestation of your intent.

When the moon reaches its fullness, meditate on what
it is that you desire and look for signs and visions of
your way into the future. Let your intention flow out
into the universe.

As the moon wanes, visualize your intention coming to
fruition for the benefit of yourself and everyone else.

give up people-pleasing

The truth is that 'people-pleasing' is a sweet-sounding name for what, to many people, actually is a serious psychological problem.

Harriet B. Braiker, author of The Disease to Please

Do you say 'yes' when you really want to say 'no?' Do you have an overwhelming need for the approval of others? If so, you're probably hiding under your 'niceness'. You have the mistaken notion that if you always think of others first you'll be protected from rejection or abuse.

By not learning how to handle difficult emotions, and by being attached to seeing yourself as a people-pleaser, you leave yourself open to manipulation. You may also be so externally focused that you lose track of your real thoughts and feelings. If you are a people-pleaser, get help to recover. Learn to balance your own needs with those of others.

63

delight in what remains

Birds sing after a storm; why shouldn't people feel as free to delight in whatever remains to them?

Rose F. Kennedy, mother of John F. Kennedy, 35th president of the United States

Life is full of human tragedies. We lose each other through death or abandonment. Our material possessions are destroyed by storm, or theft, or fire. We lose our jobs and our source of income. Disease strikes and our lives are never the same. Terrorists kill thousands in senseless acts of violence. It's no news that tragedy strikes on a daily basis. But how you respond makes all the difference.

The best response to tragedy is to celebrate what remains, even if it's only the shirt on your back. Survive adversity by delighting in the smallest things – a beautiful vase, a warm meal or the kind words of another human being.

listen to emotion

So when you are listening to somebody, completely, attentively, then you are listening not only to the words, but also to the feeling of what is being conveyed, to the whole of it, not part of it.

Alicia Silverstone, actress

To communicate well you need to listen well, and that means paying attention to more than words alone. Notice how the person you're speaking to holds their body. Do you observe any tension? Do they make eye contact in a natural way or are they having difficulty looking at you? What emotion do you sense behind their words? Is it fear, contentment, anger?

Learning to take in the whole of what is being conveyed will help you better understand what someone says, as well as become a more compassionate listener and friend.

set priorities

The important thing is to be sure you're connected with your inner compass …

Roger A. Merrill, author of Life Matters

It's not unusual to have two sets of priorities. We have wishing priorities and actual priorities. For example, you may sincerely wish to put your health and family first, but continue to eat badly and overwork. Or you may want to get out of debt, but continue to use your credit card.

Write down what you wish your priorities to be – those activities and qualities that you want to take precedence over others. Then write down a brief recap of what you did during the last week. How well are you adhering to your priorities? Asses how you spend your time. If your priorities and your reality are not congruent, start making small changes week by week. Keep track of your progress in a journal.

lower your
caffeine intake

**Widespread caffeine use explains a lot about the
twentieth century.**

Greg Egan, science-fiction writer

Our pace of life is so demanding that caffeine has become
our fuel for the 21st century. Caffeine – in the form of
coffee, tea, chocolate, over-the-counter drugs and soft
drinks – is a nice stimulant in very small doses (perhaps
the equivalent of one cup of coffee a day). The problem
comes from taking in large amounts of caffeine throughout
the day, to the point where you may become addicted. If
you stop, you may even experience withdrawal headaches.

Caffeine can affect your hormone balance and your
sleep patterns, and increases your risk of certain health
disorders such as osteoporosis, ulcers, PMT, hypertension
and heartburn. Try to cut down on your daily intake, or
cut caffeine out completely. Explore healthy ways to
energize yourself, including exercise, hydration using
non-caffeinated beverages, and taking vitamins and
herbal supplements.

share your knowledge

If you have knowledge, let others light their candles in it.

Margaret Fuller, author and transcendentalist

It's said that 'knowledge is power'. Because you live in a competitive world, you may have a tendency to hold on to your knowledge. Giving it away freely may seem foolish, when you could charge for it.

However, this mercenary approach to knowledge makes your heart miserly. Instead, share your knowledge freely – and your business and relationships will improve. By lifting everyone around you, you will benefit by having colleagues who care about you and appreciate your generosity.
You will help create a loving work atmosphere in which everyone enjoys the free exchange of knowledge. Instead of competing, you and your colleagues will be able to do your best work together and will improve both your work and your relationships.

do less of what doesn't matter

> I already knew simplicity is about power. Simplicity is the power to do less (of what doesn't matter). Simplicity is the power to do more (of what does matter).

Bill Jensen, author of The Simplicity Survival Handbook

Bill Jensen writes about simplicity in the workplace. He suggests working with management to cut down on endless meetings, inter-office email and other day-to-day time-wasters that leave you frustrated and unsatisfied with your work life. He advocates giving workers the information they need to do their jobs, and the authority to adjust that information to take care of their responsibilities.

Get together with your colleagues and see if you can suggest a way to make your work life simpler. Make a plan and present it to the management. Not all managers or business owners will be open to suggestions, but if you present your ideas as a way to improve their business your proposals may get their ear.

69

sing

Whatever the reason, be it physical, emotional, psychological
or spiritual in nature, singing is powerful.

Carolyn Sloan, author of Finding Your Voice

Do you sing alone in the car along with your radio? How
about in the shower? If you don't sing, what's holding you
back? Singing releases tension, cheers you up, lifts your
spirits and heals your soul. Singing is powerful. You don't
have to have a 'good voice' or even sing in key – just belt
out a song whenever you feel like it.

For additional fun, sing with friends. This doesn't need to
be an expensive night out at your local karaoke bar. Have a
pot-luck dinner and a 'sing-along' at home. You and your
friends can have just as much fun there, with good food, a
guitar and lots of laughter.

don't shrink yourself

Your playing small doesn't serve the world. There's nothing
enlightened about shrinking so that other people won't feel
insecure around you.

Nelson Mandela, former president of South Africa

Do you have a friend or family member who feels
diminished by your intelligence, your creativity or your
knowledge? Do you hide your abilities and talents, or stay
in the background, in order to prevent a jealous reaction
in your friends? Do you have dreams and ideas that you
keep to yourself because they may challenge those closest
to you?

The price you pay for hiding your talents is steep. You're
being dishonest in not being your true self, and you're
withholding your gifts from the world. Playing small
doesn't serve you, or your friends. Be the best person you
can be, for yourself and for the rest of the world.

affirm your completeness

Your completeness must be understood by you and
experienced in your thoughts as your own personal reality.

*Wayne Dyer, author of There's a Spiritual Solution
to Every Problem*

We live in cultures where advertising invades our lives
24/7. The message of most advertising is that you're lacking
something, and that the product being advertised will
make you whole. It's important to overcome that basic
message by meditating on your own completeness.

Find a quiet moment and close your eyes. Affirm that you
are not an apprentice human being in need of approval
by an outside authority. Affirm that you are not lacking in
beauty, health or material possessions. Affirm to yourself
that you are complete and whole. Affirm to yourself, and
the universe, that you are perfect just as you are.

work out your disagreements

Got disagreements? Work 'em out …

Paul Simon, in a song entitled 'Old', from the album You're the One

If you have serious disagreements with a friend, family or colleague, and you want to maintain your relationship, find a way to work them out. If you feel stuck, get help from a mediator – a third person whom you both trust. Be willing to understand the other person's concerns and point of view, and share your own, without blaming or putting the other person down. Express your feelings openly and encourage the other person to do so as well. It's easy to express anger, but if you're afraid let the other person know that too.

Living with underlying tension, because of ongoing disagreements, is stressful and complicates your life. To simplify your life, keep your relationships as open and harmonious as possible.

communicate in person

Electric communication will never be a substitute for the
face of someone who with his or her soul encourages another
person to be brave and true.

Charles Dickens, novelist

You probably have access to round-the-clock,
instantaneous communication by land-phone, mobile
phone and email. It's easy to put off visiting someone
when you can talk, or email, as often as you like. But it's
important to make time to see your friends and family in
person. The smiley faces and other codes you may use in
email speak volumes as to what is lacking in your 'electric
communication'. You miss the nuance in the voice, the
twinkle in the eye, the beginnings of a smile, the brush of
a hand or a good hug.

Don't rely on email and phones as a substitute for
communicating with someone in person. Make time in
your life to be with the people you love.

recycle

Use it up, wear it out, make it do, or do without.

New England proverb

The case for recycling is strong. It requires a trivial amount of your time. It saves money and reduces pollution. It creates more jobs than land-filling or incineration. It helps save trees. And recycling reduces your need to dump your rubbish in someone else's back yard. Your glass, plastic and paper are put to good use.

Get your kids involved and teach them how to sort recyclables and how to prepare them for pick-up or drop-off. Try to reuse items within your household as much as possible. Recycling is good medicine for the universe, and it makes you feel good that you're helping it to heal.

stop hurrying

Never be in a hurry; do everything quietly and in a calm spirit.
Do not lose your inner peace for anything whatsoever, even if
your whole world seems upset.

St Frances de Sales, Catholic saint

Do you rush to get places? Do you hate having to wait?
Hurrying can make you feel important and part of the
excitement of life. But these are false feelings. Hurrying
doesn't result in better productivity or help you make a
positive contribution. Instead, it makes you inefficient,
irritable, prone to mistakes, exhausted and self-centred.
You also double your odds of getting high blood pressure,
a stroke or a heart attack.

Decide to stay focused in the moment, and work on one
project at a time. Regardless of what the rest of the world
is doing, work and live at a pace that keeps you centred
and whole.

love all

Love every leaf, every ray of light.
Love the animals, love the plants, love each separate thing.
Loving all, you will perceive the mystery of God in all.

Fyodor Dostoevsky, novelist

Dostoevsky had it right: love cures all. When you are self-absorbed in your own thoughts, spending time pondering your problems or speculating on what's going to happen in the future, it's easy to forget about 'the mystery of God'.

The next time you are struggling with your emotions or trying to solve issues in your life, take a few minutes and focus intently on what's around you at that particular moment. Consciously generate a sense of love for whomever or whatever it is. See if this doesn't soften your heart, ease your worries and lift your mind beyond your everyday concerns, and towards something bigger than yourself. Let yourself merge with this larger sense of God, however you think of him or her.

grow flowers

The earth laughs in flowers.

Ralph Waldo Emerson, author and poet

Flowers have deep roots in the human psyche. We use flowers to mark our special events, such as births, weddings or funerals. We take them to friends in hospital. We give them to lovers. We grace our homes and our tables with them. We wear them in our hair and pin them on our clothes.

Get a seed catalogue and decide which flowers you love most. Then buy seeds or seedlings and plant them in your garden, on a balcony or in a windowbox. Consider both colour and scent. Grow roses, tulips and daffodils and the stately iris. Plant bulbs, flowering trees and bushes. Let flowers make your world more beautiful and fragrant. Enjoy sharing them with others.

appreciate the
basic necessities

Like when I'm in the bathroom looking at my toilet paper,
I'm like 'Wow! That's toilet paper?'
I don't know if we appreciate how much we have.

Alicia Silverstone, actress

When you hit the light switch, do you appreciate the light
that illuminates your room? When you turn on the tap and
water flows, do you marvel at having running water? When
you pick up your telephone and dial a number, do you feel
the magic when someone next door – or around the world
– says hello?

Set aside a few minutes each day to appreciate the
basics that you take for granted – from the toilet paper
to the silverware and the shoes on your feet. This deep
appreciation of the simple necessities of life keeps your
awareness keen, brings tremendous joy and ensures that
you'll never take anything for granted.

learn to sit

It is not so easy to go and sit, and even after you arrive at the
zendo and begin sitting, you have to encourage yourself
to sit well.

Shunryu Suzuki, Zen Buddhist teacher

Sitting meditation is one of the oldest forms of meditation
– and one that the Buddha taught 2,500 years ago. He
taught his followers to sit quietly so that they could calm
their bodies and minds.

Buddhist meditation is a wonderful practice, regardless of
your religion. But before you learn to meditate it's good
just to practise sitting quietly. If your days are hectic and
full of activity, or you're suffering from stress-related
symptoms such as headaches, excessive anger or addictions
to stimulants or sedatives, begin to heal by sitting quietly
for a short period every morning and evening. If this is
helpful to you, pursue formal training in meditation.

let go of perfectionism

Nearly everyone is afflicted by perfectionism to some degree, and it is easy to see it in others. The challenge is to learn to see it in ourselves.

Cynthia Curnan, author of The Care and Feeding of Perfectionists

Perfectionism is a painful habit that's easy to see in others, but hard to identify in yourself. You may celebrate your perfectionism because you think you're devoted to excellence, or just have higher standards than others. Or you may be an unconscious perfectionist as a way to ward off judgement or criticism.

If you admit your perfectionism, you may also find that you have a problem with self-acceptance. You may have difficulty regarding yourself with love and compassion. You may measure your self-worth by what you do, rather than by your qualities. To overcome perfectionism, develop kindness towards yourself and others.

81

dance

Our ancestors danced till they disappeared in the dance, till they felt the full force of spirit unleashing their souls.

Gabrielle Roth, author of Sweat Your Prayers

Dancing is free. Dance under the full moon, dance at dawn, dance at sundown. Dance naked in the privacy of your living room. Put on music and move however you want to move. That's dancing – no need for lessons, to be beautiful or have a great body, be young or talented.

Let your dance be personal and private or, if you want, communal and shared with others. Your dance can be whatever you want it to be. The main thing is to be sure to bring dance into your life. Dance at least once a week, if not daily. If you're feeling down, or stuck, it's absolutely the best medicine.

bird-watch

I hope you love birds too. It is economical.
It saves going to heaven.

Emily Dickinson, poet

Regardless of where you live, bird-watching is one of the
most frugal and funs things you can ever do.

Buy a bird feeder and hang it near your window. Fill it with
birdseed, pull up a chair and enjoy one of nature's most
beautiful displays.

Get a bird book and a notepad. Write down each species
you identify. Over time you'll get better at noticing
differences in colour and markings. If you want to attract
a wider variety of birds, find out what kind of feeder
works best for each type of bird. If you want to extend
your relationship with birds, you might want to build a
birdhouse and watch nest-building in your own back yard.
Bird-watching can be addictive, so be careful it doesn't take
over your life.

have biscuits, milk and a nap

Think what a better world it would be if we all, the whole world, had cookies and milk about three o'clock every afternoon and then lay down on our blankets for a nap.

Barbara Jordan, US senator

At first sight, Barbara Jordan's statement seems ludicrous. But, for a moment, imagine how your life would be if you stopped at three o'clock every day, had your milk and biscuits, and took a nap. If you let the idea sink in as an option for an adult, it could change your life.

In centuries past, our ancestors slept more, took their siestas at noon and had their tea at four. Some cultures still take siestas. Why not shut your office door at three, have a snack and stretch out for a little nap? If you can't quite work that out, then approximate. Bring a little sanity and self-nurturing into your day.

give gifts of service

You give but little when you give of your possessions. It is
when you give of yourself that you truly give.

Kahlil Gibran, poet and philosopher

Birthdays, holidays, weddings – these events usually require
you to buy a gift, and it's no surprise that gift-buying takes
a large bite out of your budget. A fundamental question to
ask is, 'Do I really need to give, and get, more things?'

As an alternative, consider giving gifts of service. Offer to
baby-sit, weed the garden or pet-sit while friends are on
holiday. Arrange a special outing for the kids. Try hair-
cutting, cooking, painting a room or giving a massage.
Have your close friends and family members bring a dish
to share for supper and discuss feelings about gift-giving.
Suggest that, as a group, you try exchanging gifts of service
for the coming year.

learn to exhale

Through the years I have found it wonderful to acquire, but it is also wonderful to divest. It's rather like exhaling.

Helen Hayes, actress

You could be 'turning blue' holding on to things that have outlived their usefulness. By not exhaling, or divesting, you're causing stagnant energy to accumulate in your home, and in your life.

If you show less attachment to your possessions, you'll be able both to acquire and divest easily. You'll have the sense of freedom that comes from being able to let go. You won't feel burdened and oppressed by accumulated possessions that you're not using. Look round your house for unused items and practise 'exhaling' once a month.

create the intention
for happiness

But does not happiness come from the soul within?

Honoré de Balzac, novelist

The single most important ingredient in achieving happiness is having the intention to be happy. However, creating that intention may cause some resistance. Are you used to struggling or suffering? Is that a part of your identity? If so, then putting this on the table is a good thing. It's time to acknowledge this and let it go.

Sit down and write a list of 30 activities that make you feel happy. Intend to be happy today by doing one of those activities. For example, if smelling flowers fills you with joy, bring some happiness into your life by visiting a botanical garden or buying yourself a bouquet.

87

take a yoga class

The postures and breath work that you do in a typical yoga class will change your life.

Katrina Kenison, author of Meditations from the Mat

Creating a simpler and more spiritual life will help you slow down, reconnect with your body and improve your health and well-being. Yoga is a wonderful practice for accomplishing all of the above.

There are many ways to find yoga classes and instruction. Try your phone book for listings of yoga studios and schools. For less expensive classes, try your local college, church or neighbourhood school. If you really want to save money, search YouTube for yoga videos and follow the actions as you watch. Or find a book at your local library and try teaching yourself. You may want to purchase some inexpensive props, such as blocks, mats, belts and blankets.

explore herbal remedies

The first herbal guide dates back five thousand years, to the Sumerians, who used herbs such as caraway and thyme for healing.

Earl Mindell, author of Earl Mindell's New Herb Bible

Herbs have been used by all cultures for millennia for healing and disease prevention. Overall they're safer than synthetic drugs, but they're potent medicine and should be used responsibly. All you need is a little information and common sense.

Read up on any herb that you are considering taking. Stick to the recommended dosage, and watch for allergic reactions or interactions with other herbs and drugs. Used carefully, herbs offer inexpensive and effective remedies for many everyday illnesses, such as the common cold or flu.

learn about your chakras

By examining your relationship to the different powers and sacred truths inherent in each chakra, you can learn more about where you need to focus your attention and clear out energy blockages.

Carolyn Myss, author of Carolyn Myss's Journal of Inner Dialogue

Chakra is a Sanskrit word that means 'wheel'. According to ancient knowledge, we have seven chakras, or energy centres, in our body. The three lower chakras are associated with primary needs, such as survival, money and procreation. The four higher chakras are associated with love, communication, knowledge and wisdom.

Your chakras can easily become blocked through stress, or negative thinking, and your symptoms may manifest as physical ailments. For example, if you are having trouble expressing yourself, you might have problems with your throat chakra, which could manifest as thyroid problems.

By learning about your chakras, you can understand the best way to keep your energy flowing freely and your chakras unblocked.

follow your conscience

We all struggle at times to know what to do to seek and abide by our conscience. The outcome of these struggles affects the course of your life, and the lives around you.

Bill Shore, author of The Light of Conscience

Bill Shore is the founder of Share Our Strength, an American non-profit-making organization that has raised more than £55 million ($100 million) to support anti-hunger and anti-poverty organizations worldwide. Share Our Strength has mobilized tens of thousands of individuals to contribute their talents towards anti-poverty efforts.

Consider what you can do to help end hunger and poverty in your town, or in the world at large. Any contribution of your time and effort – however small or brief – will help. When you respond to injustice, you act in harmony with your conscience, and in so doing you may change your life.

use up your leftovers

The most remarkable thing about my mother is that for thirty years she served the family nothing but leftovers. The original meal has never been found.

Calvin Trillin, essayist

What do you do with the leftover ingredients from making a recipe, or with the leftovers from dinner? You may have good intentions and dutifully save them, but in a few days they may find their way into your rubbish bin. You then end up not only losing the food, but losing your hard-earned money as well.

Your problem may be that you just don't know how to use that leftover rice, that half cup of green beans or the rest of the tomato paste. Try reading a cookbook on using up leftovers (ideally one that lists foods by name, and then suggests recipes for their use) for ideas about how to utilize leftovers in creative ways.

learn simplicity
from others

Finding out who we really are and what we truly want is perhaps best discovered by learning about others who are in the process of doing the same.

Linda Breen Pierce, author of Choosing Simplicity

In her book, Linda Breen Pierce reports on her three-year study of 211 people who simplified their lives. Their experiences will give you the courage to move forward in your own quest for simplicity.

Not everyone chooses to simplify their lives in the same way, or starts from the same place, or has the same goals. It's important to find role-models that reflect your own particular situation. Reading about other people's experiences is a great way to get ideas for your own life, as well as to avoid the pitfalls they encountered along the way.

don't get discouraged

One of the things I learned the hard way was that it doesn't pay to get discouraged.

Lucille Ball, comedian

Life is not easy. Problems arise on a daily basis. Success in one area of your life may be met with defeat in another. You may have started your own business and failed miserably. Or you may have written your first novel, only to be met with a stack of rejection letters.

Whether you're an optimist or a pessimist doesn't change the fact that life is difficult. The antidote to the reality of life is to not entertain discouragement. No matter what happens, keep your optimism intact. Stay active and keep your faith in yourself.

create your own
sand mandala

---

*Art [...] is well accepted as a precious window into an
alternative reality, into the enlightened dimension.*

*Marylin M. Rhie and Robert A. F. Thurman, authors of Wisdom
and Compassion*

In Buddhism, the word mandala means 'circle'. Sand
mandalas are forms of ritual art depicting sacred
mansions, or the homes of particular meditation deities.
Some monks use brightly coloured sand to create the
highly complicated mandala.

Both the deity and the mandala itself are considered
manifestations of the Buddha's enlightened mind.
The mandala is created with an understanding of
impermanence and non-attachment. After it has been
completed, it is eventually swept up and deposited in a
river. Explore making your own sand mandala as a prayer
for your own healing.

find your true passion

Your true passion should feel like breathing; it's that natural.

Oprah Winfrey, talk show host

Look for your passion in unlikely places. Do you love beautiful fabric? Do you enjoy museums and art? Are you the one who livens up the party with your sense of humour? You may have buried your passions in a nine-to-five job, and are discounting your interest in fabric, art or humour as being irrelevant to your life.

For one month keep a note of everything that really excites you – no matter how impractical, insignificant or even grand it seems. This list is a key to your passion: the things that light you up and make you forget to eat. Then begin to honour your passions and bring them to the centre of your life.